OUR STREET

OUR STREET

ANNE FORSYTH

Illustrated by Robert Geary

Scripture Union
130 City Road, London EC1V 2NJ.

© Anne Forsyth 1991
First published 1991

ISBN 0 86201 719 X

All rights reserved. No part of this publication may be reproduced, stored in a retrieval system, or transmitted, in any form or by any means, electronic, mechanical, photocopying, recording or otherwise, without the prior permission of Scripture Union.

The right of Anne Forsyth to be identified as author of this work has been asserted by her in accordance with the Copyright, Designs and Patents Act 1988.

Phototypeset by Intype, London
Printed and bound in Great Britain by Cox and Wyman Ltd, Reading

Contents

Tim   7

Mick   17

Mandy   26

Tessa   36

Sam   43

Kevin   51

All together now!   60

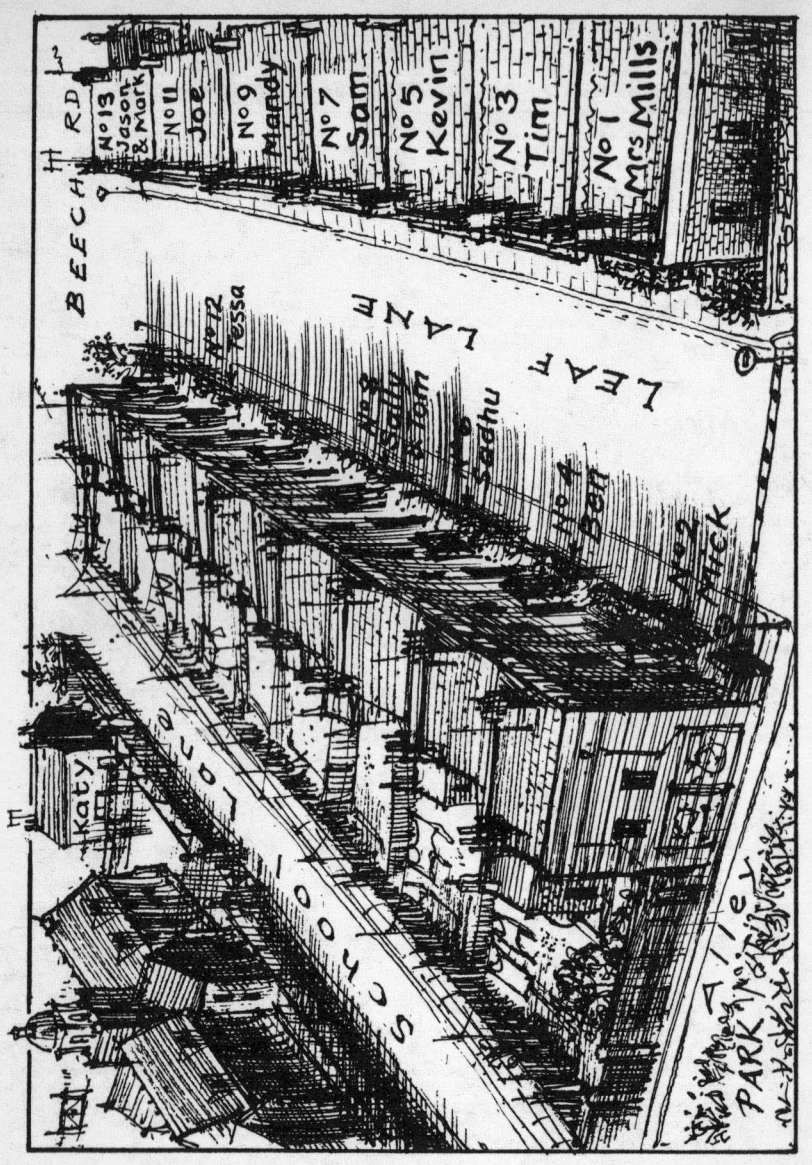

Tim

'I wish we could go home,' said Tim.

He looked out of the window at Leaf Lane. It was so very different from the country. It was quiet, a small backwater of a street tucked away from the main road. It was quiet because no one ever went through Leaf Lane in a car. At one end there was a narrow passage which led into School Road, with a barrier to stop you riding a bike through the alley. At the other end was Beech Road, which wasn't busy either. It was a wide road lined with trees. It was wide enough for lots of learner drivers to practise there.

Mum looked up from the books she was unpacking. 'I know it's different, but we'll soon settle down. It's such a friendly street.'

Tim said nothing for a moment. He kicked the leg of a chair and scowled. It was a miserable slushy February day. What a time of year to move house!

And there was nothing happening outdoors. Back home in the village it had been different. They had lived right on the main street. There was always something exciting going on.

'There's no one my age!' he burst out.

Mum sat back on her heels and looked up at him. 'Now that's silly,' she said. 'There are lots of children in Leaf Lane. You'll soon make friends – and you'll get to know the other boys at school. And the children in Leaf Lane do lots of things together. Someone told me the whole street goes carol singing at Christmas.'

Tim refused to be cheered up. 'Christmas is months away,' he grumbled. 'I liked it where we were.'

He was determined to sulk. He knew it made things miserable for other people but he didn't care.

'Oh, stop complaining, for goodness sake,' said Mum. Then she said, 'Sorry, I didn't mean to snap. Come on, give me a hand, will you – we'll move these empty boxes into the garage.' She put her arm round him. 'This is a nice town with lots to do. Dad's got a good job and we like the house. You're bound to feel a bit strange at first. But you know,' she went on, 'God helps us. When we're feeling a bit sad or lost, he's there, no matter where we live.'

But Tim was still cross. What was the use of asking God to help, he thought. He wouldn't change things back again and let Mum and Dad and Tim return to the village where they'd lived for years.

Tim gulped as he thought of the village and the people he'd known. There was his friend, Paul, and the rest of the family at the farm. There were the next door neighbours, and the people at the village post office, and of course all the boys at the village school.

Tim was tall for his age. He'd been the strongest in the whole class, and he could run faster than anyone else. He'd been a bit of a leader, really, he thought. And now, he wouldn't be important any more. He'd just be one of a group. How would the football team get on without him?

He remembered how miserable he'd felt, saying goodbye, and how they'd all said, 'Come back and see us.'

Well, they meant it, didn't they? Suppose, Tim said to himself, I was to go home. Mum can't *make* me stay here.

That night, when he went to bed, he thought it over. Mum had said, 'God always listens to us. He's always there when we tell him about things that are troubling us.'

So Tim asked God, 'Please help me to get back to our village.'

Then he turned over and tried to go to sleep. But it was very different here. In the village, it had been so quiet at night, that you could hear the rustling of the leaves, and now and then a dog barking. Here there was the sound of traffic from the main road, a few streets away, and sometimes the sound of a car door banging, or cars changing gear at the corner.

He woke up in the middle of the night. It was all dark, and everyone else was asleep. He lay for a few minutes wondering, in a sleepy sort of way, why everything felt so unreal. And then he remembered. It wasn't real, here in the town. It was real back home in the village, where he'd come from.

Suddenly it was clear to him. I'll go back, he said

to himself. I could stay at the farm. I wouldn't cost very much to feed. And I could go back to school. Hadn't Mrs Walters said when he left, 'We'll miss you, Tim.' She'd be pleased to have him in the class again.

He began to feel a lot happier, and he turned over, feeling drowsy. I'll work it out in the morning, he promised himself. But I'll go back, the sooner the better.

Next morning, when Dad had gone to work, Mum said, 'I've got some food shopping to do and I need a new mop and more curtain hooks and things like that. We'll go into town.'

'All right,' said Tim. His thoughts were still a long way off – he was thinking about his great plan.

It was a small town and very friendly. Shop assistants smiled at Tim and his mother, and chatted and hoped they'd be happy in their new home. It was the same at every shop – at the baker's, the fishmonger's, the ironmonger's.

Back home, Mum unpacked the shopping and made a cup of coffee. Tim gazed moodily out of the window. Just then, the doorbell rang. On the step was a boy about Tim's age, holding a football. 'Do you want to come to the park?' he said. 'We've got a football team in our street – you can join if you want.'

'No,' said Tim very firmly, not even adding 'thank you.' He wasn't going to play with a lot of kids in a street game. After all, he'd been the best goalkeeper the village school had ever had.

'Tim,' said Mum, 'that wasn't very kind. You

won't make friends that way.'

'I've got other things to do,' said Tim, and he stamped off upstairs.

While Mum was busy, he looked out his clothes. He would need an anorak and jeans, and a couple of shirts, and the thick sweater that Gran had bought him. He'd need money too. Did he have enough money for the fare? He'd no idea how much it might be.

He counted out his money. There wasn't very much. He'd have to ask Mum for next week's pocket money, and maybe a bit extra. He'd say it was to buy cars for the model garage.

Tim didn't say any more to Mum about being homesick for the village. He found out that there was a bus that went to the railway station and asked Mum for his pocket money in advance. She gave him two weeks money and didn't ask any questions. That night he secretly packed his haversack. He was really looking forward to going back to his old school. He was glad he didn't have to start going to a new school next week among a lot of strangers.

So next morning, when Mum was busy, he took a couple of apples from the fruit bowl, and a bar of chocolate he'd bought the day before.

Just before he set off, he wrote a note explaining that he was going back to the farm, and he'd stay with Paul and go to the old school. He put the note on the desk in his bedroom.

'I'm going to play outside in the garden,' he shouted to Mum.

And he closed the door behind him and set off

along Leaf Lane towards the main road and the bus stop.

He had just turned the corner into Beech Road, when he saw the girl. He knew her by sight already – she was the sister of the boy who had asked him to play football. The brother and sister were very much alike, both with freckles and red hair.

But today something was wrong. Usually the girl looked cheerful and sang as she skipped along the street. But today her face was all red and she looked as if she had been crying.

She rushed up to Tim. 'Oh, please help me – he's lost, our pup! He was on the lead, but he started pulling and chasing after another dog and I couldn't hold him. He's lost!'

'What's he like?' asked Tim.

'Black, with floppy ears. He's only small,' – and she looked as if she were going to cry again.

'It's all right,' said Tim. 'I'll help. Which way did he go?'

'He ran along the Lane, then into Beech Road,' she explained. 'His name's Chips –' and she started to call the dog. But there was no sign of the little black puppy.

'Come on,' said Tim. 'Let's look for him.' Together they set off down the Lane.

They looked into front gardens and kept calling and whistling.

'Don't get so upset,' said Tim, trying to cheer up the girl a little. 'He hasn't been gone long, has he?'

'It seems ages,' she said, her tears beginning to well up. 'It's the first time he's escaped, and It's all my fault.'

Tim didn't know what to do. Then he had an idea. 'Let's go back to your house. Then your brother could come and help us look.'

'That's an idea!' she brightened up. 'He's good at finding things.'

'You'll be going to our school,' she said. 'It isn't far, only in the next road.'

'Yes,' Tim nodded. He'd quite forgotten for the moment that he was carrying a haversack and setting off for the village. He was going back to his old school. But just for the moment, the missing puppy seemed much more important.

'We live at number eight,' said the girl.

'And we're at number three.'

'I know,' said the girl. 'Oh, what am I going to tell Mum?' She looked really upset until Tim said, 'What's that?'

'Where?'

'At your door – you said number eight.'

'It's Chips!' The girl's face broke into smiles, and she rushed up to her front door. 'You clever dog! You found your own way back!' The pup jumped up, still trailing his lead, all wriggling black body and pink tongue.

She picked up the pup and hugged him to her. The door opened and a smiling woman stood on the doorstep. 'What's all the excitement about, Sally?'

'He ran away and found his own way back – isn't he clever? Oh, and this boy helped me to look for him.'

'And what's your name?' asked Sally's mother. 'It was good of you to help.'

'It's Tim,' he began, and before he could say any more, Sally's mother invited him indoors, saying how kind he had been and wouldn't he come in and have some juice and biscuits.

'No, really, it wasn't anything,' he said, and he forgot all about how miserable he'd been and was really pleased for Sally and her family. But then he said, remembering, 'I must go home and tell Mum where I am.'

'Of course you must,' said Sally's mother. 'She'll be worried if she doesn't know.'

Tim did hope he could throw away the note he'd written – just imagine if he *had* caught the bus and then the train, and gone running back to the village!

'Oh, there you are!' said Mum, as he opened the door. 'I was just coming to ask if you wanted to go to town with me.'

'Not today,' said Tim, and he explained all about Sally and the little black pup.

Before he went back to number eight, he rushed up to his room – the note was still there, and he tore it into little pieces.

That evening Dad said, 'Saturday tomorrow. What do you want to do? Go to the swimming baths?'

'Actually,' said Tim, 'I'm going to be busy. Sally and Tom have got this great little dog – it's nearly as clever as old Tess at the farm. We're going to teach it to "sit" and "stay" and do tricks.'

That night, Tim added a bit to his prayers. 'Thank you, God, for my friends,' because there was Sally and her brother Tom and Chips and the children's mother, who had made him feel really welcome. Wasn't it funny meeting Sally like that? What a good thing that God knew best and hadn't sent Tim back to the village but had answered his prayer in a different way.

Tim yawned. It was all rather too much to think about tonight. And there was a lot to do tomorrow. So he just said, 'Thank you' again, and turned over and went to sleep.

Mick

'That boy!' said Tim's mother, and she slammed the window. 'I've never heard anyone with such a loud voice. I wish he'd be quiet.'

Everyone agreed that Mick had the loudest voice in the street. You could hear him when he was playing football, or when he was calling to a friend. You could hear him when he was arguing with his elder brother, or just when he was talking in an ordinary voice. He never stopped shouting.

'That boy!' said old Mrs Mills, who lived at the end of the Lane. 'He always seems to be fighting with someone.'

She was right, of course. If there was a fight in the street, Mick was right in the middle of it. He wanted to be the best swimmer, the fastest runner, the best centre-forward. He wanted to be top of the class in everything. He wanted to shout at everyone, 'Look at me!'

'The trouble is, he's the one in the middle,' said Mick's father.

Mick had an elder brother who was good with his hands, and who was popular with everyone.

And he had a small sister who still needed lots of care.

'I suppose it *is* difficult being the one in the middle,' said Mick's mother, and she tried to explain to him that being the one in the middle didn't matter. He was important too.

But Mick didn't listen. He just went on shouting. You had to be very careful what you said to Mick. Tim, who was new to the Lane, was careful not to argue with him. Tim was tall and strong, but Mick – well, he was short and square and very very tough. He didn't often lose a fight.

All the same, Tim was quite good friends with Mick, who lived across the road at number two. In fact, Tim had made quite a lot of friends, and he didn't feel nearly so strange now.

But Mick had one special friend – Sadhu. It seemed odd to people that Mick had a friend like Sadhu, who was very gentle and quiet and never needed to fight anyone at all.

'Good thing they're friends, those two,' said old Mrs Mills. She noticed quite a lot about the street, although she never walked much further than the park around the corner, where she would sit and read, or just enjoy the sunshine.

Every day Mick would call at Sadhu's house on the way to school – Sadhu lived at number six.

'I'm off, Mum!' Mick would shout, and slam the door so hard that the whole house seemed to rock.

One spring Saturday morning, Sadhu went round to his friend Mick – Mick's house was the last one in the Lane, and Sadhu went through the back gate as he always did. This morning he had a new kite – it was a fine, breezy day, and he wanted to go over to the park to try it out.

Almost at once, Mick opened the back door. When he saw Sadhu, he didn't say anything at all, which was odd for a start.

'Look what I've got! It was a present. Coming to the park to try it out?' said Sadhu.

Mick just looked at him. 'No,' he whispered. Yes, that's right – he *whispered*.

Sadhu looked at him in astonishment. 'What's the matter?'

'Nothing,' said Mick, still whispering. 'Just you be quiet, eh? I'll come over to the park this afternoon. Got things to do this morning.'

'Oh, all right,' said Sadhu, who was quite puzzled by all this. 'But what's wrong? What are you doing?'

'Just watching,' said Mick. 'That's all.'

'Your mum, is she all right?'

Mick nodded.

'Well, then,' said Sadhu, 'what's the matter? What are you watching for?'

'Nothing's wrong, I tell you,' whispered Mick. 'Just you go on without me. And if you see the milkman, tell him he's not to go clinking the bottles when he comes to our house. And anyone else you see, tell them they've got to be very quiet when they're passing our house.'

'I wish you'd tell me,' said Sadhu.

'Can't tell you anything yet,' said Mick. 'You tell one person, you tell everyone. They'll all want to be tramping along here. See you later.'

Sadhu was really astonished and he felt rather

angry. After all, he hadn't done anything but be a friend to Mick, who didn't have many friends.

Maybe Mick was ill. Maybe there was trouble in his family. Then Sadhu had an idea. He'd ask old Mrs Mills, later on, when he went along with her magazine. Sadhu's mother passed on her weekly magazine to the old lady. Mrs Mills was very wise and knew a lot about everything, although she didn't go far from home.

As Sadhu crossed the Lane, he met Kevin. 'Is that your new kite?' asked Kevin. 'You coming to the park?'

Sadhu explained that there was something rather odd about Mick. 'I think there's something wrong.' He was worried. Maybe Kevin would be able to help.

But Kevin had no idea what might be the matter with Mick. He thought he'd mention it to his friends, Jason and Mark, who lived at number thirteen, at the other end of the Lane.

The family were finishing a late breakfast. Kevin sat down and drank the orange juice his friends' mother poured out.

'Mick's gone very peculiar,' he said importantly. 'I think there's something hidden in their garden.'

'Oh, nonsense,' said his friends' mother.

But the story travelled, all the way down the Lane. 'Mick's got something hidden in his garden.' The story grew and grew. Someone actually said that Mick's big brother, or was it his dad, had brought home a silver trophy, and buried it in the garden, and Mick had been told to keep watch. And they weren't letting anyone into the house.

Going on the afternoon shift, Mick's dad smiled and waved to the neighbours as he always did. He wondered why some of them didn't wave back.

Sadhu's mother opened the window. There were quite a lot of children in the street today, but no Mick. 'Oh, isn't it quiet without that voice!'

Later on, Sadhu went along to Mrs Mills, to hand in her magazine. She was knitting and watching the television with the sound turned down.

'Hallo, Sadhu,' she said. 'Just turn the TV off, will you?'

Sadhu sat down and watched her for a moment or two. Then he said, 'There's something wrong with Mick.' And he told the old lady the whole story.

'Oh!' Mrs Mills started casting off stitches and counting to herself, as if she weren't paying any attention. But Sadhu knew she was listening hard.

'He's not speaking,' said Sadhu.

'You mean he's fallen out with you?'

'Not that. He's whispering. And so quiet – he doesn't bang doors any more.'

And he told her how Mick had forbidden anyone to come near his garden.

'What a change!' The old lady smiled. 'Poor Mick. He does feel he has to be important and show off about it.'

'And what's more,' said Sadhu, 'they're even saying that Mick's dad might be a jewel thief, and maybe the jewels are hidden in the garden.'

'Who on earth made up that nonsense?' said Mrs Mills, still counting stitches.

'You see I told Kevin, and Kevin told . . . '

'. . . someone else. That's how silly stories spread.' She was very quiet for a moment, and Sadhu knew she was thinking. She was very wise, the wisest person he knew, but she always said she wasn't wise at all. It was just that she asked God all the time about what she should do, and he helped her whenever she had a problem.

'I don't think,' she said, her eyes still on her knitting, 'that your friend is a thief. Nor his father. Nor his brother.'

'Oh,' said Sadhu. She sounded quite definite about it, and he supposed she must be right.

'I don't think there's a lot of valuable silver buried in the garden. But I do think there's something there. Something – or someone – he wants to protect.'

It all sounded very mysterious. Sadhu rather liked mysteries. He enjoyed working out puzzles.

Someone there? Someone hiding from the police, maybe? Or a spy?

'But,' he said, 'why is he whispering like that? He wouldn't say. He just wanted me out of the way.'

'I think,' said Mrs Mills, finally casting off the stitches, 'putting two and two together, I'd say there's nothing very mysterious about it at all. I'd say your friend Mick is learning how to look after something or someone. I think God is showing him how to be gentle, instead of always bullying and bragging. If you go back to see him, instead of listening to the stories that people spread, you might learn the secret.'

So Sadhu went back to Mick's house. Certainly everything looked normal. He knocked at the back door.

Mick appeared. 'Hallo,' he said in a perfectly friendly way, although he was still whispering.

'Can I help . . . ' Sadhu began, and then he laughed. It was catching. He was whispering too.

Mick began to laugh, then he stopped himself. He glanced over towards the hedge.

'If I show you something,' he said, 'will you promise to be very very quiet?'

'Promise,' whispered Sadhu.

'OK then.' Mick led the way across the grass to the hedge. Carefully, he parted the leaves. 'See,' he whispered.

Sadhu looked into the hedge. There was a nest all neatly made from bits of straw and leaves and twigs – there was even some fluff and a bit of sticky tape that must have blown into the garden. Inside the nest were four young blackbirds.

'If we wait,' said Mick softly, 'the mother comes and feeds them.'

The two boys stepped back and watched from the other side of the garden as the mother blackbird returned to the nest. From the distance the boys could hear a faint chirping.

'Let's go inside now,' whispered Mick.

Once they were indoors, he explained in his normal voice, only not quite as loud as usual, 'I'm going to look after these birds. If people shout or crash about, they'll disturb them. The mother might not come back. So we've got to be very quiet – understand?'

Sadhu nodded. He was fascinated by the nest. 'Can I come back tomorrow and have a look?'

'Of course you can,' said Mick. 'As long as you're quiet.'

When Sadhu next called on Mrs Mills, he told her, 'It's a bird's nest – in Mick's garden.'

'I thought it might be something like that,' she said.

'You're like a detective,' he said.

The old lady laughed. 'No mystery about it. I've been watching the blackbirds build their nests every spring for a very long time. I just thought your friend Mick might be learning how to care for something or someone weak and helpless. Just as God looks after us, so we must care for his creatures. He is glad when we all learn how to be kind and caring.'

'Even Mick,' said Sadhu with a grin.

'Even Mick,' she agreed, smiling back at him.

'All the same,' said Sadhu, 'he won't let anyone harm these birds. Know what he said? "If anyone scares them, I'll thump him." '

'I think he would too!' said Mrs Mills.

Mandy

'We're doing a play at the end of term!' Mandy was bubbling over with excitement. 'It's about a beautiful princess in a fairy-tale castle.' Her eyes sparkled. 'I'd love to be the princess. We've all got to read a bit and then Miss Brown will choose the best.' She went on: 'I'm much the best at acting. Better than Sally. She giggles a lot. Better than Charlene.'

'Who's Charlene?' Mum looked up from the ironing board. She was finishing off a new skirt she'd been making for Mandy. She pushed open the window. It was a warm, early summer day. How much quieter it was in Leaf Lane now. Had that boy Mick moved, or was he less noisy than he used to be?

She smiled at Mandy. 'I haven't heard you mention Charlene before.'

'Her mum and dad have the café next to the paper shop – you know, on the High Road. They live up above the café.'

Mandy could hardly sleep that night for excitement. Next day she skipped all the way to school, thinking about the play, and the costume she'd wear. She could see herself in a white, floaty sort of dress, with a shining tiara. Not real diamonds, of course, but they'd look real in the stage lights.

And Mum would make her dress. She was really clever at dressmaking.

Mandy very badly wanted the part. That night, she added a bit to her prayers. 'Please, God, let me be chosen.'

Next morning, when she got to the playground, there was a little group of girls by the gate. She could see Laura and Joanne and Gloria, who were all her friends. She ran up to them. 'Hallo!' she called.

And then she stopped. They were all gathered round Charlene and she was telling them something funny.

It wasn't fair, thought Mandy. Charlene was good at everything – good at lessons, good at games, and she was popular too. She could tell wonderful stories in that gentle voice and she could make people laugh.

But Mandy didn't hear what she was saying. And she didn't even listen when her best friend, Lucy, ran up, all out of breath. 'I nearly missed the bus,' she panted. 'Mum was up all night with the baby, and we overslept.'

Mandy was thinking about the play. She went on thinking about the play all through the morning. She knew she could look like a princess – she was tall, and she was proud of her long fair hair. 'You're too proud,' said Lucy once. 'Always thinking about yourself.' They hadn't spoken for two whole days.

Just before dinner time Miss Brown said, 'All those who'd like to be in the play, I want you back here at half-past one . . . '

There was a specially good dinner that day. Mandy liked apricot crumble and it was hard to choose between that and her favourite jelly with fruit. But today she could hardly eat anything for excitement. She imagined going home that afternoon, telling Mum about the play, planning her costume. She thought about the performance itself, and how Mum and Dad and her big sister, and maybe Gran, would all come along to watch.

'Now I want you to read page three,' said Miss Brown, 'starting at the first line. I'll read the other parts. Remember she's a beautiful graceful princess, but in this scene, she's really afraid. She doesn't know what's going to happen.'

Several of the girls had come along to read. There was Penny, and Joanne – oh, and Charlene. Mandy didn't listen to any of the others reading. She was too busy planning how she would walk and how she'd sit down very gracefully, and how she'd speak the lines.

When it came to her turn, she put everything she'd got into the part. She was grand, and then bewildered and afraid . . .

'Good, thank you all for reading,' said Miss Brown. 'Now I'll think about it, and let you know later this afternoon, and we'll start rehearsing right away. I want this to be the best play we've ever done.'

Mandy didn't pay any attention to the lessons

that afternoon. Later on, she saw Miss Brown coming into the classroom, and her heart began thudding with excitement. This was her big moment.

'Now I've chosen who will play the main parts,' said Miss Brown. 'But, as I've told you, there will be a part for everyone. First, the princess. Charlene, I'd like you to play her . . . '

Not Charlene. She *couldn't* play the princess. It must be a mistake.

'Mandy, I'd like you to play the woodcutter. He's a very funny character. I know you'll do it well.'

A woodcutter! Even a funny one! It wasn't the same as playing a princess.

At the end of the afternoon several girls ran up to Charlene congratulating her. But Mandy walked away on her own.

When she got home, Mum was baking for a coffee morning. Usually Mandy liked to help, to cut the biscuit dough into fancy shapes. But this time, she just flung her bag into the corner, and slung her anorak over the banisters. She was about to go upstairs when Mum called, 'How did you get on today?'

'All right.'

'Can't hear you,' said Mum. 'Want some juice?'

'I said "all right".' Mandy put her head round the door. 'No, thanks, I don't want anything.'

And then she said, all in a rush, 'I didn't get the part of the princess. It's not fair. Charlene got it. And I'm far better than her . . . ' Two big tears welled up.

'Oh, I'm sorry.' Mum shook the flour from her hands, and wiped them on a cloth. She gave Mandy a quick hug. 'I know it's disappointing, but there will be other plays. Have you got a part?'

'I'm the woodcutter.' Mandy sniffed. 'It's not much of a part.'

That night, Mandy didn't feel like saying thank you to God. What was there to thank him for? She'd asked him to let her play the princess and he hadn't listened.

Mandy was angry about it. 'And now I'll have to watch *her* playing the part.'

Next week, rehearsals got under way. Everyone helped – mothers were asked if they'd lend a hand with the costumes. Mandy's mother was always in demand. She could run up costumes very quickly and was good at finding bright remnants of material for next to nothing.

Still, Mandy couldn't bring herself to be nice to Charlene. She knew she ought to say, 'Congratulations. You'll do well.' But she couldn't.

She got caught up in the excitement, however, and did her best to make the woodcutter a funny character, and she was pleased when Miss Brown said, 'Well done! That's just how I want it.'

But still there was that niggling feeling. And anyway, Mandy didn't want to play a comic character. She wanted to play the princess.

One day there was no rehearsal at dinner break, because Miss Brown was off school with a heavy cold. Most of the girls were in the playground. It was nearly time for the bell to ring and Mandy remembered that she'd left her library book in the cloakroom. There was just time to get it and take it back to the school library before the bell rang.

There was no one in the cloakroom. Yes, there *was* someone sitting there, huddled in a corner. It was Charlene.

Mandy felt a little embarrassed. She tried to creep out. And then she turned back, because she heard a little sniff, and what sounded like a sob. There was no doubt about it. Charlene was crying.

Suddenly Charlene looked up.

'What's the matter?' said Mandy before she remembered that she wasn't really speaking to Charlene.

Charlene gulped. 'It's my mum. She's got to go into hospital and she won't be here for the play. I was looking forward to it so much, and her helping to make my costume, and coming to see me...' and she gave another great sob.

Mandy didn't know what to say. Suddenly she felt very ashamed of herself. She sat down beside Charlene, and said, 'I'm sorry about your mum. It's a shame she can't come to the play. You'll be really good as the princess.' She was a bit surprised when she heard herself say that, but she knew it was true.

On the way home, she thought very hard. She remembered what Gran often said. 'God shows us a way if we really ask him.'

So she asked him then and there. 'Please show me a way to help Charlene, and make her mum better soon.'

As Mandy got home, her mother came in from the garden. Right away, Mandy poured out the whole story. Then she said, 'Could you help with her costume? Please!'

'Of course I will. You tell Miss Brown tomorrow. I'm glad you want to help Charlene, and I'd love to work on her costume.'

But there was something else. Mandy couldn't forget Charlene crying in her disappointment. She had so wanted her mother to be there to see her in the play.

And Mandy thought, 'How would I feel? How would I feel if I'd got the part, and there was no one there from my family to clap, and say, "You did well", and be proud of me?'

So she said to Mum, 'You'll all come, won't you? To see Charlene in the play, I mean. We could sort of be her family – or she won't have anyone there.'

'That's a great idea,' said Mum. 'After all, God wants us to help one another and to share in the good times and bad times.'

So that was all right. Mandy began to feel much happier. The miserable feeling she'd had for ages began to go. Mum smiled at her and she felt just a happy as if she *had* got the part of the princess.

Being part of a family was the best thing of all, she knew. That night when she said her prayers, she said she was sorry about being jealous and nasty, and she said a special thank you for her own family because they loved her and had enough love to share with other people.

She remembered Gran saying that God shows us another way, and from then on she did as much as she could to help Charlene.

She heard her lines and helped Charlene to

remember the bit she always forgot when she began to get nervous.

Mum went round to see Charlene's father and told him she'd make the costume and help all she could. Charlene's father was very grateful.

'I can't leave the café,' he explained. 'If my wife had been here ... '

Charlene's dress was finished in good time for the dress rehearsal. It looked just as Mandy had imagined it, but better. It had a lovely shiny bit down the front, a piece of braid that Mum had picked up in the market.

With her dark hair and glowing eyes, Charlene looked every inch the princess. 'Ooh, I'm scared,' she said to Mandy as they stood in the wings.

'Don't be, you'll be great,' said Mandy, and she really meant it. She found herself asking God to help Charlene and see that she didn't forget her lines.

Then Mandy went on as the woodcutter. She was surprised and pleased when people laughed.

Best of all, she could see her own family, right in the front row, all smiling and clapping and wanting Charlene to do well.

At the end Charlene and the rest of the cast took their bows. The curtains were drawn and they all went off the stage. Now they began chattering.

'I nearly forgot to curtsey.'

'There's a pin sticking into me.'

'Did you see how I nearly tripped?'

'You all did very well,' said Miss Brown. 'And especially Charlene.'

Charlene's eyes shone. 'My family came to see

me,' she said. 'Well, Mandy's family actually . . . '

Mandy's mum came backstage. 'I just popped into the café,' she said, 'before the play began. And there's great news. Your mother's getting home at the end of the week, Charlene.'

Charlene smiled. 'It's been a wonderful evening.'

'Wasn't she good?' said Mandy, and to her surprise, she really meant it.

Tessa

'Go on, say it again!'

The little group of girls clustered around Katy.

'What was that you said?' Donna giggled. 'A wee while?'

Katy flushed. 'There's nothing funny about the way I speak.'

'Aboot the way Ah speak.' Donna, the leader of the group, rocked with laughter. She kept saying over and over again, 'Aboot the way Ah speak.'

'Scuse me,' Katy muttered, and she rushed away from the group, tripping over a kerb, and banging her elbow against the door in her hurry to get inside school.

'I hate it here!' she said that evening to Mum. 'They laugh at me because I'm different.'

'Oh dear, that's very unkind,' said Mum, giving her a quick hug. 'The best thing to do is pay no attention. They'll soon get tired of teasing you.'

'I wish we could go back home,' Katy burst out. 'I liked living in Glasgow. I don't like it here.'

And she gave a gulp as she remembered all her friends in Scotland. It seemed such a very long way off. And everything was so strange here in the south of England, and joining a new school in the summer term was even harder, somehow.

'If only I had a friend,' she thought, 'someone to talk to.' But everyone else at school seemed to be in such a close group. They had jokes she didn't understand and they all talked so quickly.

Tessa had joined in the laughing and teasing – just at first. Tessa was always laughing and joking – people down Leaf Lane, where she lived, called her 'that bright little girl'. So, to begin with, she had joined in the jokes about Katy and her funny accent. And then – she watched Katy pushing her way through the group, and suddenly felt a bit uneasy. Some of the girls were still giggling and shouting 'Cowardy custard!' after Katy.

How would I feel if that was me? Tessa thought. If I went to live somewhere else and people laughed at me because I was different? I'd feel so unhappy I'd want to run away.

So she very nearly turned round and said to Donna, 'You stop that. It's not kind.'

Very nearly, but not quite. Donna was really clever, and so pretty, with dark curly hair. She was popular – the teachers liked her because she always answered questions, and was ready to read in class or run messages or take part in sponsored silences or whatever the class was doing.

So she must be all right, mustn't she? Everyone liked her. If *she* thought it was fun teasing – well, it was quite harmless. It didn't mean anything, and gave everyone a good laugh.

That was what Tessa told herself as she walked home that afternoon.

Anyway, if she tried to stop them teasing Katy, 'Well, they might turn on me,' she said to herself. And that would be terrible. She couldn't bear it if she wasn't allowed to join in the skipping and the games in the playground.

'Hallo!' called Mandy from across the road. Mandy and Tessa were quite good friends. Tessa had once thought that Mandy was stuck up and much too pleased with herself, but she seemed a lot nicer these days. However, Tessa didn't stop to talk. She just waved and pushed open the door of her own house, number twelve. She was still thinking.

That night she was very quiet and didn't eat much at supper time.

'Anything wrong?' asked Mum.

Tessa just shook her head. All that weekend, she kept thinking about Katy. She tried asking God what she should do. She knew how kind and loving he was. She was sure he would want her to help Katy. But she wasn't at all clear what to do. It would be so dreadful to be an outcast – and yet . . .

On Sunday evening, Aunt Josie came along for supper. Tessa liked it when Aunt Josie called in at her house. She often popped in on her way into town. She was very cheerful and laughed a lot and had hundreds of friends. Everyone in the town seemed to know her. She was always helping people, and Mum said she did lots of kind things that no one ever got to hear about.

While Mum was making the supper, Tessa suddenly thought, 'I'll ask Auntie.' So she said, all in a rush, 'Auntie, did anyone ever laugh at you?'

Auntie stopped smiling and looked serious. There was a pause, and then she said, 'Yes, they did. Do you know, I'd almost forgotten. It was such a long time ago.' She gazed into the fire, as if she were seeing something in the past.

'It was the bright blue stockings,' she said. 'In those days, we all wore stockings to school, black stockings with navy gym tunics.'

Tessa nodded. She'd seen pictures of Auntie in the middle of the hockey team, looking very smart.

'Well,' Aunt Josie continued, 'it was war time, and it was very hard to get clothes and wool – everything was rationed. I was given a pair of bright blue stockings – I think they came in a parcel from America. I can't remember. Nowadays, they'd look really smart and trendy – ' She looked at Tessa's red and orange socks and laughed.

'But in those days we all wore black stockings and we all wanted to look just like everyone else. And my mother insisted I wear the stockings to school. It was wasteful otherwise, she said. I kept tucking my legs underneath the desk and hoping no one would notice.

'I remember,' she went on, 'it was at break time. You could see my bright blue stockings a mile away and one girl pointed to them and laughed.'

'What did you do?' asked Tessa.

'Nothing I could do,' said Auntie. 'I had to wear them. Anyway, I remember how miserable I felt. I thought everyone was laughing.' She paused. 'And then – there was one of the girls, a quiet little thing – no one ever paid much attention to her. She said suddenly, "I think they look nice." It took quite a lot of courage to stand out against the crowd when everyone else seemed to be laughing. God helps us there,' she added. 'He gives us the courage if we ask him. It's much easier to be one of the crowd. Like the people who lined the streets to watch Jesus on his way to the cross. It was so much easier and safer to stand by than to stand up for him.'

Tessa was rather silent after that. But she thought about Aunt Josie's story as she walked to school next morning. And she asked God to help her and to give her the strength to stand up for what was right, not just to be one of the crowd.

Katy was already in her place in the classroom. She was very quiet and kept her head bent down.

At breaktime everyone rushed outside. Donna, who always seemed to have lots of pocket money, had bought a new skipping rope the previous Saturday.

'Let's have a turn,' said someone.

'Of course,' said Donna generously. She was like that — very generous, very willing to share things. 'Come on, Katy — what about you? "Gie's a turn — gie's a shot" — isn't that what you say?'

Everyone began to laugh. 'What's the matter?' asked Donna, looking at Katy's flushed face. 'You're not going to cry, are you? "Greeting" — that's what they call it where you come from, so my mum said. You're not going to greet, are you?'

Suddenly, Tessa, who was on the outside of the group, felt her face getting warmer, and something bubbling up inside. She pushed her way into the centre of the group.

'You stop that!' she shouted at Donna.

Everyone turned and looked at Tessa.

Donna said, 'What do you mean? Don't you speak to me like that!'

'You stop teasing her. It's cruel making fun of the way she speaks. How would you like it if someone did that to you?'

Donna looked very surprised. One or two of the others looked a bit shamefaced. Of course they'd laughed at Katy, but it was only a bit of fun, wasn't it?

'I never meant anything,' muttered Donna.

'It's bullying!' Now Tessa was wound up, she couldn't stop. 'If I ever hear you being nasty about her again, I'll – I don't know what I'll do,' she finished.

'All right, I'm sorry. I didn't mean it,' said Donna very quickly. 'Look, Katy, why don't you have first turn on my rope.' It was her way of saying, 'I'm sorry.'

Later Tessa sat down beside Katy at the table where they were drawing autumn leaves. Katy grinned. She was rather shy, and Tessa knew this was *her* way of saying 'thank you'.

Now that niggling miserable feeling disappeared altogether. Tessa felt happy again and she said a little thank you to God for helping her.

On the way home, she walked along with Katy. Katy wasn't nearly so shy now. She told Tessa all about Glasgow and about her cousins who lived on a farm in the Highlands and about the great holidays she spent there.

'My house is on Beech Road, just along here,' said Katy.

'We're in Leaf Lane – number twelve,' said Tessa. 'You could come round to my house. See you tomorrow.'

Tessa bounced along the road and into number twelve. That evening she felt so much happier.

'What are you smiling about?' asked Mum. 'You look really pleased about something.'

'It's nothing,' said Tessa. 'Nothing really. I was just thinking about a pair of blue stockings.'

Mum looked puzzled. 'Oh?'

But Tessa wouldn't say any more.

Sam

It all began with such a silly little thing.

Joe said, 'Can I read your comic after you?'

But Sam said, 'No, you can't.'

Usually Sam was good about sharing things, but on this particular day he was feeling cross.

Joe looked rather surprised. He and Sam had been friends for a long time. Their families were good friends too. Sam and his family (Mum, Dad, his brother, Peter, who was a year or two older, and his big sister, Liz, who worked in an office in the town), lived at number seven Leaf Lane. Joe and his family were at number eleven – Joe, his mum and dad, and the baby.

Joe's mum and Sam's mum would help each other with shopping. And Joe's dad was always willing to lend a screwdriver or a pair of pliers to Sam's dad.

So they all got on very well. But after that matter of the comic, Sam and Joe weren't such good friends as before. Joe thought, 'Well, if he likes to be mean, let him', and didn't bother calling for Sam next morning as he went to school.

Next day Sam walked home from school on his

own. He stopped, as he sometimes did, to buy a comic and to spend his pocket money on sweets. Usually Sam and Joe would have spent a long time deciding what to buy, and they would share the sweets they bought. But this time, 'It's all for me', Sam thought, and he was secretly rather pleased. By the time he had finished all the sweets he felt a little queasy, but he told himself that it didn't matter.

Then again, it seemed funny not having anyone to joke with. Joe had the biggest appetite in the whole street, and Sam the next biggest. He was always hungry — it was a bit of a joke between them.

That evening, after supper, which he didn't enjoy as much as usual, he sat down to read his comic. But it didn't seem quite as funny this week.

Of course Sam and Joe still spoke to each other. They would play football in the park or catch the same bus to the swimming baths. But Sam found that he rather liked being on his own. When Mum gave him an extra apple or piece of fruit loaf in his lunch box, he didn't need to share it as he used to, but ate it all by himself.

'Tomorrow morning,' said Mum, 'I really must sort out things for the earthquake appeal. We've lots of good woollens and there are blankets too.'

Sam wasn't really paying attention, so he was a bit surprised next morning when the doorbell rang and there on the step was Tessa, from number twelve, carrying a huge cardboard box. Behind her was another girl — someone Sam didn't know.

'Blankets,' said Tessa. 'And my friend Katy's

brought lots of jerseys.'

'Oh, that is kind!' said Sam's mum. 'What lovely blankets – and really warm jerseys. Thank you!'

The two girls went off chattering and laughing, all the way up the Lane, and Sam's mum turned to sorting out the woollens.

'They're for the appeal,' she said, when Sam asked. 'At church we were asked to give woollens and good clothes and blankets for those poor people who have lost their homes and are cold and miserable.'

Sam's mum was collecting from all the people in the Lane. His big sister Liz had given some clothes, and Peter had given some shorts that he hadn't worn much, so they were still quite good.

'Toys, too,' Mum went on, 'for the children who haven't anything at all. They've lost everything. You've got some things you could send, haven't you? Toy cars – and farm animals. You're too old for them now.'

'No,' he said slowly, 'I haven't anything to give.'

'We all have something to give,' said Mum. 'God wants us to share with those who haven't anything. We have plenty, so we must help those who haven't as much as we have.'

'Well,' Sam muttered, 'I'll see.'

But when he looked through his old toys, there was nothing he wanted to give. The farm animals – maybe he didn't play with them now, but they were really good ones. Why should he give them away to some child he'd never seen? And his cars – well, some of them had lain in the bottom of the box for a long time. But he'd spent money on them.

He'd saved up his pocket money to buy them, so why should he give them away?

Later on, Dad was about to deliver the boxes to the church hall.

'You got anything to give, Sam?'

Sam shook his head. 'I don't think so.'

All these things are mine, he said to himself. But somehow, he didn't feel all that happy about it.

'Oh,' said Dad, surprised, 'that's greedy. That's not like you, Sam.' And he didn't say anything more.

A few weeks later, one fine Saturday morning, Sam's dad said, 'How about a picnic by the sea?'

Everyone in the family agreed that was a very good idea. Sam said he'd take a bat and ball for rounders, and a spade. His brother Peter said he'd take swimming trunks just in case it was warm enough to swim. Dad said he'd take the garden chairs. Mum said she'd take a book and some cushions to lie on. And Liz went off to find the suntan lotion.

Mum made rolls filled with ham and lettuce, and put in some hardboiled eggs. She packed apples and oranges and fruit cake and biscuits. Dad made the coffee and poured it into a flask and Sam packed the cartons of juice. Peter read out the weather forecast from the paper. 'It's going to be warm and sunny all day,' he said.

They all got into the car, Mum and Dad and Sam and Peter and Liz, who was wearing her dark glasses and suntan lotion already.

The traffic was nose to tail all the way to the sea,

because lots of other people had read the weather forecast and decided they'd have a day out. Dad began to get a bit grumpy, so Mum said she'd drive for a bit. Then Dad lost the way and there was an argument.

However, as they came over the crest of the hill and saw the sea all sparkling in front of them, everyone forgot to be cross and said again what a beautiful day it was.

When they got to the beach, they managed to find a spot that wasn't too crowded. But all the same, there seemed to be hundreds of other people on the beach, all shouting and playing rounders and building sandcastles and splashing in the sea.

The family unloaded the chairs, the bat and ball, the swimming things, the magazines, the spade and the cushions.

Dad peered into the boot of the car. 'Where's the picnic basket?'

'It's in the boot,' said Mum. 'You put it in.'

'No, I didn't. I left it to you.'

'Well, I left it to you. You were loading the car. Look again.'

So Dad looked and Sam looked and Peter looked and Liz looked.

They all looked into the boot of the car, but there was no picnic basket.

'Left behind!' said Mum.

'Are we going to starve?' asked Sam anxiously. He didn't like to be without food for more than half an hour.

'Course not,' said Dad crossly. He went on, 'We can buy food to eat.' They looked round. There

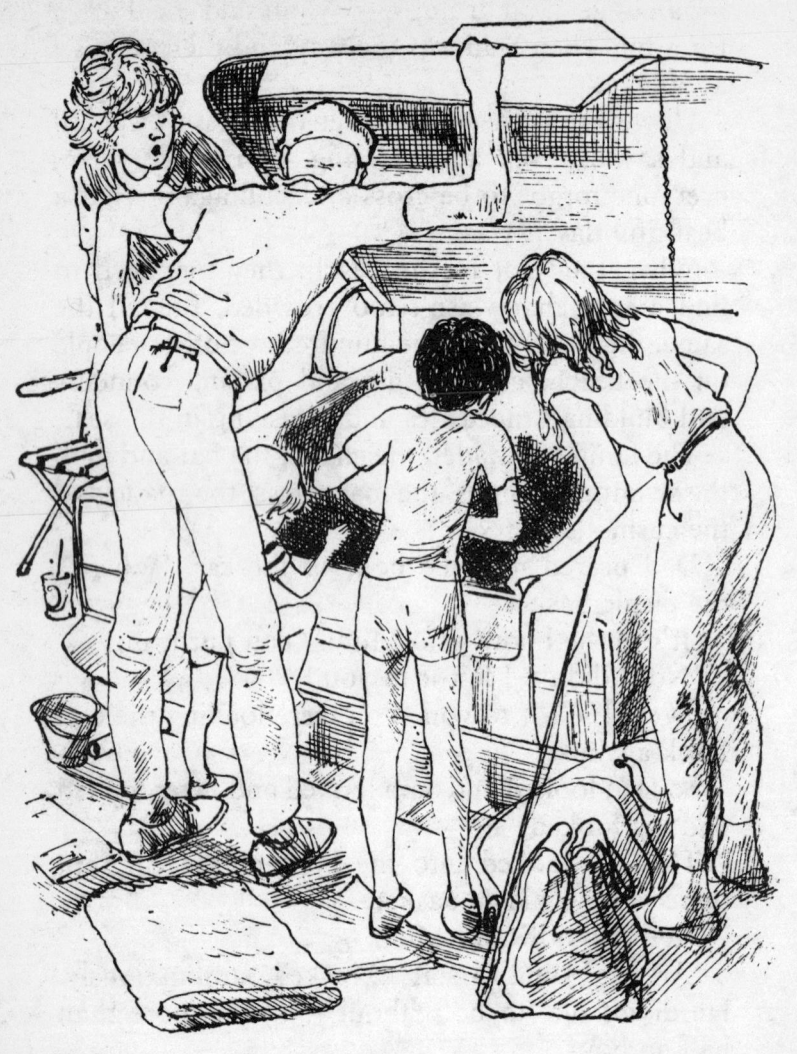

was nothing in sight but a kiosk. They went across to it, but found it sold only ice-cream and soft drinks.

'Not enough to keep us going,' said Peter.

'And very expensive,' said Dad.

And anyway, there was a long queue.

'Well, I'm going to sunbathe,' said Liz, and she stretched out on the sand.

'Anyone want to play rounders?' said Sam, but no one did. So he wandered down to the edge of the sea. 'Don't get lost!' called Mum.

Maybe, he thought, he could build a sandcastle or a fort, or watch the people flying kites, or the windsurfers.

Oh, he did feel hungry! He tried not to think about it. I wish I had a ham roll and a big piece of fruit cake, he said to himself.

'Hey, careful!'

'Oh, sorry!' He had nearly tripped over someone else's sandcastle.

'No harm done,' said another voice, then, 'Hallo – what are you doing here?'

It was Joe's dad – and there was Joe, and his mum and the baby. Sam was so surprised to see them that he forgot he and Joe weren't really friends.

'We're at the seaside, that's what we're doing,' he said.

'I know that,' said Joe. 'Wouldn't mistake it for anywhere else, would you?'

'Don't be so rude,' said Joe's mum.

But Sam just grinned. He was used to Joe's teasing.

'We've just got here,' Sam told them, 'but I think we're going off to find something to eat.'

'Didn't you bring a picnic?' said Joe's mum.

'We did, but it got left behind. We forgot the picnic basket.'

'Oh, you poor things,' said Joe's mum.

Then Joe chipped in, 'We've got plenty. They can have some of ours.'

'Of course you can,' said Joe's mum warmly. 'There's plenty of coffee and juices too. Tell your mum to come over here and we'll share it all out.'

'Well,' said Sam's dad later on, 'we really are very grateful to you.'

It was surprising how far the sausage rolls and sandwiches and bananas and cake went among so many people. Everyone seemed to have enough to eat, and the fruit juice and coffee went round too.

Sam felt really ashamed. Joe had shared his food without saying, 'It's mine. I'm keeping it for myself.' Sam began to feel bad about the way he had behaved – about refusing to give Joe a look at his comic, and keeping all his sweets to himself, and even worse, not wanting to help the appeal. Sharing made you feel much happier. He remembered how Mum always said, 'There's plenty for everyone in God's world, if only we learn how to share.'

Then he had a brilliant idea. 'Our picnic's at home. When we get back, you could all come and help us eat it.'

'Right!' said Joe.

Kevin

'I wish he wasn't coming,' said Kevin. He rubbed his hands through his hair and it stood up on end. Kevin was probably the untidiest boy in Leaf Lane. He brushed his hair now and then, his laces were always untied and he looked as if he had just thrown his clothes on. But he didn't have time to bother about things like that. He was too busy building models and inventing things.

'I wish he wasn't coming,' he said again.

His mother paid no attention. She just went on, 'So you must be very quiet and as helpful as you can. And you don't mind moving out of your room, do you? It's only for a week or so.'

'Yes, I *do* mind,' said Kevin, and his face got very red.

'Kevin!' said his mother, 'That's not a bit like you.'

Kevin didn't say a thing. He flung out of the house and went across the street to see his friend, Ben, who lived at number four.

'It's not fair!' he burst out. 'We've an old uncle coming to stay. Mum says he's been ill, and he's got to have my room.'

'Have you to move out?'

'I've to sleep on a camp-bed in the sitting room, and I've to move all my things. It's not fair – why can't he go somewhere else, and why does it have to be *my* room?' He scowled.

'Hard luck,' said Ben. 'I wouldn't like someone coming to stay in *my* room.' He looked around at the posters and model aircraft and books. 'I don't think anyone could get in,' he said honestly. 'It's a bit of a mess.' Ben was always trying something new. One week, he'd be making a kite, the next week he'd be studying insects. The trouble was, he never finished anything.

'And I've to be very quiet,' Kevin went on. 'Quiet and tidy and not have the TV on loud, so that he can have a rest. Why can't he go somewhere else?' He was so annoyed that he didn't want to look at the model of a Cessna plane that Ben's aunt had brought him.

'Maybe *he'll* bring you something,' said Ben.

'No, he won't. He's poor. That's why he's coming to stay with us, instead of going away for a holiday.' Kevin felt really cross.

Look at his friends, Sam and Joe. They didn't have to have elderly uncles to stay. No one else had to move out of their rooms.

Kevin scuffed his shoes along the pavement as he went back to number five.

Inside, Mum was getting ready for Uncle Alf's visit. And a few days later, when Kevin came back from school, there he was, sitting in the best chair by the fire. He was an old man with white hair and a smiling sort of face. But he looked pale and rather thin.

'This is Kevin,' said Mum. 'You haven't seen Uncle Alf for a long time. You were just a baby when he last came to stay.'

'Pleased to meet you,' said the old man.

Mum had made a special chicken pie for supper. And there was apple sponge to follow, which was Kevin's favourite. But tonight, he didn't feel like eating.

'You're not eating, Kevin,' said Mum a little sharply. 'Anything the matter?'

Kevin just shook his head.

Uncle Alf enjoyed his meal. 'We'll soon build you up again,' said Mum, smiling at the old man.

After supper, Kevin got up from the table. 'Back later,' he said.

'Where are you going?' asked Mum.

'You're not going out, are you?' said Dad.

'Just across to Ben's.'

'All right then,' said Mum. 'Don't be late.'

Well, they needn't think he was going to stay around talking to this stranger. And he couldn't get into his room to work on the model ship he was making. 'You needn't move the model,' Mum had said. 'Uncle Alf won't mind.'

It wasn't fair.

'How long is he staying?' asked Ben that evening.

Kevin kicked moodily at the leg of a chair in Ben's room. 'Don't know. Don't care much.'

He knew he was being awkward and difficult. But if they had to have visitors, why not someone young, not this old man.

That night, Kevin didn't have a lot of things to thank God for, the way he usually did. This time, he thought God was being very unfair. After all, Kevin thought, I've tried to be kind and help Mum and not grumble. But here was Uncle Alf staying in Kevin's house and Kevin's room, and there was no chance of getting into the room for ages, even to work on the model of the sailing ship. 'I *did* want to finish it and show it to Ben,' Kevin said to himself.

For the next few days, things were fairly quiet. Uncle Alf sat in his chair and read or slept and sometimes watched television. In the evenings, he would play chess with Dad, or sometimes have a game of Scrabble with Mum. Every day when Kevin came home from school, Uncle Alf would ask how he got on. But Kevin wasn't prepared to be friendly. He'd just say, 'Oh, fine,' or 'OK, thanks,' and leave it at that.

Sometimes Kevin would catch Mum looking at him in a puzzled sort of way. But he pretended not to notice.

One morning, Mum said, 'Would you mind going round to the paper shop for Uncle Alf? He wants a big notebook and a couple of ball-point pens.'

'Can't he go himself?' said Kevin.

'I don't think I heard that,' said Mum. 'I'll go.' And she walked out, ignoring Kevin.

Kevin felt all miserable inside, but he was sure he was in the right.

After all, it was *his* home, wasn't it? He hadn't asked Uncle Alf to come and stay. So why should he act as an errand boy?

Kevin was spending more and more time at Ben's house, just across the way at number four. This Saturday morning everyone was getting ready for a family celebration. An aunt and uncle were having their ruby wedding party at Ben's house. The house seemed to be full of people laying tables and putting out sausage rolls and flans and salads and all sorts of sweets. And right in the middle of the table was a splendid iced cake.

Surely, thought Kevin, they'd ask him to stay to the party. He really did his best to be helpful, giving Ben a hand to carry chairs, and fetching things for Ben's mother.

He stayed on, and on, all through the morning. He knew his mother might wonder where he was, but he didn't care. Let her wonder.

Then Ben's mother said, 'Perhaps you should be going home, Kevin? Won't your mother be worried? Maybe you'd like to pop over tomorrow and have a bit of cake.'

So he wasn't to be asked to stay. Gloomily he crossed the street, wondering what was going on at his house. There was sure to be a row, or a cold sort of silence anyway. Kevin knew he'd been rude and unhelpful.

But at lunch time, Mum was her usual self. She didn't pay any attention to Kevin. She dished up bowls of soup and brought in a large plate of filled rolls, without asking Kevin to help.

The next morning Kevin decided he would take his model sailing ship over to Ben's house. They could work on it together – there was plenty of space.

He knocked at the door of his bedroom, then pushed the door open. 'Please can I . . .' and then he saw that Uncle Alf was standing there, the model ship in his hands.

'Don't you touch it! It's mine!' Kevin burst out.

Uncle Alf turned round, and immediately Kevin saw how frail he was, and felt a little ashamed. But all the same . . .

'It's *my* ship – I'm working on it,' he said.

'I'm sorry,' said the old man, 'Shouldn't have touched it.'

'It doesn't matter,' said Kevin, and he rushed out of the house, and stood on the pavement outside, wondering what to do. He'd spend the day at Ben's anyway, he thought. So he crossed the street and rang the doorbell.

'Oh, hello, Kevin, you're up early,' said Ben's mother, and she yawned. 'Ben's not up yet. Do you want to come back later?'

'Could I – er – come in and wait?'

'Well, yes, if you like.'

So Kevin followed Ben's mother round the house, and Ben's sister, Tracey, helped too. They carried plates and tidied up the sitting room and vacuumed the bits of crisps and pieces of sausage rolls from the carpet.

'I'm making a cup of coffee. Anyone else want one?' Ben's dad put his head round the door. 'Lovely morning – we've been right round the park.' Pip, the family mongrel, launched himself on Kevin. He seemed to be full of energy, though everyone else looked a bit sleepy.

Sitting at the kitchen table with a mug of coffee, Ben's father leaned back in his chair. 'Ah, that's better.'

He took another sip. 'Before I forget, Kevin, tell your Dad I'd like to pop across and have a chat with your uncle one evening. I didn't know till the other day that he was staying with you – nor that he was your uncle.'

'But how do you know him – ?' Kevin was puzzled.

'He taught me, years and years ago,' said Ben's father with a smile. 'Taught me woodwork at school. He's a real craftsman. You should have seen the beautiful furniture he made. I'd like to talk to him again. We learned a lot from Mr Smith. He's a fine person.'

Kevin was very quiet after that, and he went home in a little while. He was thinking hard.

Uncle Alf wasn't just a frail elderly man who was taking up space in Kevin's house. He had been a good teacher, someone the boys looked up to, a real craftsman. That's what Ben's father had said.

And suddenly he very much wanted to make up to Uncle Alf for being so unkind. Kevin asked God to help him, and he knew the very first thing he must do was say he was sorry.

He gulped and walked straight into the house and up the stairs to his – to Uncle's room, and knocked on the door before he had time to think about it.

'Come in,' said Uncle Alf.

'I'm sorry I was rude,' said Kevin, all in a rush.

'I'm sorry I meddled with your things. I know I didn't like people interfering when I was your age. It's a fine model, though, and you're making a good job of it.'

'I'd a bit of trouble with this part, just here,' said Kevin, picking up the model ship. And he found himself explaining the difficulty to Uncle Alf.

And Uncle Alf said he didn't want to take over, but maybe the piece marked G went in like this. And sure enough it did.

Somehow, after that, Kevin got to know Uncle Alf quite well and it didn't seem a bother having him to stay. Before long, Kevin was bringing his friends round to see Uncle Alf. When you got to know him, he was great fun, full of jokes and stories.

So it came as a bit of a surprise when Uncle Alf said it was time he was going back to his own flat, and he felt so much better for his stay.

'You're not going home already! Don't go!' said Kevin, and he really meant it. Mum smiled and Kevin felt things were all right again.

'Well, you'll come back and stay, won't you?' said Kevin, and Uncle Alf promised he would. 'After all, I've promised to make that desk for you and the shelves for your room – yes, I'll be back.'

All together now!

'Everyone ready then?' said Ben's dad.

It was Christmas Eve, and the children of Leaf Lane were going carol singing as they did every year. Ben's dad was in charge. He kept everyone in time and made sure no one wandered off.

Tim jumped up and down in the clear frosty air. It was going to be a super evening. He grinned at Mick. He and Mick and Sadhu had become good friends. Someone said that Mick had nearly been put out of the carol singing last year – not just because he had such a loud voice, but because he started fighting with one of the boys from along Leaf Lane. And you can't have people fighting and singing carols.

There were Tom and Sally, Sally beaming all over her face. And there was Tessa – she'd brought her friend Katy, who didn't live in the Lane but round the corner. 'She's never been carol singing before,' Tessa explained to Ben's dad.

'Yes, I have,' said Katy, 'where we used to live.'

'Well, not down here. We're the best singers in the town,' said Tessa in a bossy way. Not that Katy seemed to mind.

'My word,' said Ben's dad. 'You had better be good this year . . . '

Sam and Joe were there. They were just as close friends as they'd ever been, and did everything together. Ben hadn't meant to come – he had so many things to do at home. But it *was* Christmas, and you couldn't miss the carol singing.

Mandy was there. She kept getting the words of the carols mixed up with the words she'd been learning for the Nativity play at school. This time she was a shepherd, and she had a really good costume that Mum had made from an old woolly dressing gown and two tea towels. Somehow it made Christmas a lot more special having a friend like Charlene to share things with. This time she was helping Mandy to learn *her* words.

Kevin looked along the Lane to his own window. He could see in the window the beautiful crib that Uncle Alf had built. And he knew that Uncle Alf was making something else – a surprise present for Christmas. He wondered what it was.

'Now,' said Ben's father. 'All ready? Let's begin with *Good King Wenceslas* . . . '

Of course you could hear the children all the way along the Lane, because it wasn't a very long street, and everyone was singing. Mandy had brought her recorder too, and she played a solo verse of *Silent Night*.

People put their lights on, and lots of houses had Christmas trees in the windows, so the whole Lane seemed to glow.

The children moved along the street, singing outside each door. Tom and Sally took their collecting can to every house. The children were collecting for a village in Africa, to help build a well, so that everyone would have clear, fresh water to drink.

When they reached the end of the Lane, there was Mrs Mills in her doorway.

'Any special requests?' called Ben's dad. 'What would you like us to sing?'

'*Away in a Manger*, please,' Mrs Mills said. 'That's my favourite.'

So they sang all the way through *Away in a Manger*.

'Lovely,' said Mrs Mills. 'Now come inside.' Indoors she had piping hot mince pies, and hot drinks and a bright fire, and everyone rubbed their hands, and said they weren't cold really, and wasn't it a good thing it was such a fine starry night.

As they left, Tim looked up at the stars. Well, he thought, it was very different from the country – very different, but what a lot of friends he had made. He looked round them all. He couldn't believe that he had been so miserable when they had first moved to the Lane.

Tessa thought about Katy and how much better things had been since she and Katy had become friends.

Sam and Joe didn't think about anything very much. They were too busy munching the last of the mince pies. Mrs Mills had said, 'I can't possibly eat all those – not on my own. Take some with you.' Both Sam and Joe felt pleased that they were friends – and it wasn't likely that they'd ever quarrel again. It was much better to share things, thought Sam.

Kevin thought about Uncle Alf, and how much he was looking forward to Uncle Alf's Christmas visit. He couldn't believe he hadn't wanted Uncle Alf around.

Mandy thought about her friend Charlene – it was good to have a special friend like her.

Mick thought about the nest in the garden – he'd enjoyed taking care of the fledglings. And somehow fighting didn't seem as much fun now. But there were lots of things to do with his friends – he grinned at Tim and Sadhu.

As Mrs Mills closed the door, she said a special thank you to God, because although she lived alone, she wasn't lonely. She had lots of friends, all down Leaf Lane.